Your

# DUI Handbook

## The Citizen's Guide to Your DUI
## in Pinellas County

Russo Pelletier & Sullivan

ATTORNEYS AT LAW ◆ DUI & CRIMINAL DEFENSE

### Timothy F. Sullivan, Esq.
### Marc N. Pelletier, Esq.

# Free Consultation
## 727-578-0303

www.duistpetersburglawyer.com

9721 Executive Center Drive North
Suite 120
St. Petersburg, FL 33702

3000 Gulf to Bay Blvd.
Suite 100
Clearwater, FL 33765

# Table of Contents

# Introduction

The facts and circumstances of every DUI case are unique. For that reason, you should never rely solely on books or the internet. When facing a DUI charge it is imperative that you contact an experienced attorney who can properly investigate all of your defenses, formulate a strategy, and seek the best possible result.

If you intend to hire a DUI attorney to protect your best interests and your driving privilege, you should carefully consider the attorney's training, skill, and qualifications. We are former state prosecutors who only handle DUI cases arising out of Pinellas County. We understand how the system works. We are in court nearly every day. We continually deal with the same judges and the same prosecutors. Put our experience to work for you.

Dealing with a DUI charge can be a stressful and challenging experience. We invite you to explore the helpful information in our DUI Handbook that was authored by the DUI defense team at Russo Pelletier & Sullivan. The following pages may answer many of your immediate concerns and provide you with a better understanding of your options.

# How to Emotionally Survive a DUI

No one ever wakes up in the morning and decides to commit a DUI offense. This charge is different from most other crimes because the prosecutor need not prove a criminal intent. A DUI arrest typically follows the exercise of poor judgment, as opposed to a deliberate and conscious decision to violate the law. In other cases, clients may not have been driving while they were impaired, although they may have had a moderate amount of alcohol earlier in the evening. As a result, they are charged with a crime that they did not commit because law enforcement "made a bad call" after the traffic stop.

### You are Going to Get Through This

We counsel clients that a first time DUI offense, absent serious injury or death, is not a felony or a crime involving untruthfulness or dishonesty. Yet, people charged with a first-time DUI offense can often be "hard on themselves." They regret the conduct that resulted in their arrest. The stress caused by their arrest can weigh heavily on them and result in sleepless nights.

Last year, there were 61,852 arrests for DUI in just the state of Florida. If you were arrested for a DUI, you are certainly not alone. Although this is a serious charge, "it is not the end of the world." Together, we are going to get through this problem.

## A DUI Arrest Can Happen to Anybody

Over one million people are arrested each year for DUI in the United States. This has included many notable people. However, it is important to remember that in the overwhelming number of cases, getting arrested for a DUI offense did not serve as an impediment for their success in both their professional and personal lives:

President George W. Bush
Vice President Dick Cheney (Twice)
Tim Allen (Comedian & Television Actor)
Reese Witherspoon (Actress)
Charles Barkley (Professional Athlete)
Diana Ross (Entertainer)
Sam Donaldson (National News Anchor)
William Levada (Catholic Cardinal)
Wynonna Judd (Entertainer)
Nick Nolte (Actor)
Tracy Morgan (Twice) (SNL Comedian & Television Host)
Robbie Knievel (Motorcycle Daredevil)
Michael Phelps (Twice) (Olympic Athlete)
Carlton Fisk (Baseball Hall of Famer)
Bobby Dale Earnhardt (Race Car Driver)
Crystal Davis (Eastern Kentucky Police Chief)
Tiger Woods (Golfer)

## Taking Steps to Address Your Anxiety

Clients worry if their arrest will appear in the local newspaper. They contemplate the embarrassment they will suffer if their friends or family members learn about the incident. They typically express concern that their DUI could jeopardize their employment, result in a jail sentence or cause their privilege to drive to be suspended.

 If you have been arrested for DUI, you may be experiencing fear, shame or humiliation. It is normal to experience some anxiety. However, you are likely to gain a greater peace of mind by meeting with a qualified DUI defense lawyer to answer your immediate questions. You can take advantage of significant insight from a defense lawyer who has first-hand experience with the Pinellas County Criminal Court system. We will be in a good position to evaluate the chances for a reduction of your DUI charge to the lesser offense of reckless driving. We can tell you which Judge is assigned to your case and what you can expect.

 Another way to effectively cope with stress is by keeping busy. We can teach you the proactive steps that you can take right now that will likely save you time and money in connection with your DUI charge. We can determine whether we can keep you driving without interruption, as well as, educate you on the topic of hardship licenses.

We have helped thousands of people charged with DUI. Spending time with us at a free consultation could remove some of the weight from your shoulders and enable you to get your life back on track.

*Let Your Arrest & Concerns Become Our Responsibility.*

# The First 24 Hours - 4 Crucial Steps

The first 24 hours are critical to minimizing additional costs associated with your arrest, protecting your privilege to drive, avoiding social media exposure, and preserving evidence that may later be beneficial to you and your attorney. The first chapter of this book is designed to provide guidance on the critical steps that you should immediately take.

 ### 1. Get Your Car Back

After being arrested for DUI, the police officer has the discretion to choose one of three methods to deal with your motor vehicle:

- In some cases, the arresting officer will ask you if a sober friend or relative can arrive within twenty minutes to pick up your car.

- If your car is in a secure location and parked in a lawful manner, the arresting officer may simply lock your car and leave it, to be retrieved by you later. Your car keys will be returned to you with the rest of your personal property when you are released from the Pinellas County Jail. To determine the location of your vehicle, you need simply refer to the document charging you with DUI (your criminal arrest affidavit), which will reflect the location where you were arrested.

- In many cases, the arresting officer will have your car towed by a wrecker to a tow yard. It will remain stored there until such time as you pick it up after your release from the Pinellas County Jail. If your vehicle was towed, it is important to act quickly. Not only will you be charged a fee for the towing service, but you will accumulate storage fees for each day the car remains in the lot. This is an example of a "hidden cost" the government has imposed on people arrested for DUI.

## How Do I Locate the Pinellas Towing Company That Has My Car?

Each police agency has a contract with local towing companies that they call on a rotation basis. When you were released from the Pinellas County Jail, you may have been given information regarding which towing company is in possession of your automobile. If you were not given that information, you should call the police agency that arrested you and inquire which towing company was responsible for recovering your automobile. Below is a list of Pinellas County Law Enforcement agencies and their administrative non-emergency phone numbers:

| | |
|---|---|
| **St. Petersburg Police Department** | **727-893-7780** |
| **St. Pete Beach Police Department** | **727-582-5721** |
| **Clearwater Police Department** | **727-562-4242** |
| **Pinellas Park Police Department** | **727-369-7864** |
| **Largo Police Department** | **727-587-6730** |
| **Tarpon Springs Police Department** | **727-938-2849** |
| **Gulfport Police Department** | **727-582-6177** |
| **Kenneth City Police Department** | **727-498-8942** |
| **Treasure Island Police Department** | **727-547-4595** |
| **Pinellas County Sheriff's Office** | **727-582-6200** |
| **Pinellas Sheriff's North District Office** | **727-582-6900** |

## Questions to Ask the Towing Company

After securing the name of the towing company, you can use our list below to contact them. We recommend that you:

◉ Confirm that your vehicle is in fact being stored at that impound lot;

◉ Obtain the total amount due for services rendered associated with the towing and storage of your vehicle; and

◉ Inquire as to what form of payment is accepted.

# Towing Companies Under Contract with Law Enforcement

| | |
|---|---|
| **Tri-J Towing & Recovery** <br> 125 19th St. S. St. Petersburg <br> (727) 822-4649 | **L&J Auto Service** <br> 5790 Park Blvd. Pinellas Park <br> (727) 544-2233 |
| **Sunset Point Towing** <br> 1920 Sherwood St. Clearwater <br> (727) 469-8999 | **Gulf Coast Auto Body & Service** <br> 7201 Gulf Blvd. St. Pete Beach <br> (727) 367-2171 |
| **Leverock's Towing & Transport** <br> 4750 95th St. N. St. Petersburg <br> (727) 391-3577 | **Clearwater Towing Service** <br> 1955 Caroll Street Clearwater <br> (727) 441-2137 |
| **Yoho's Auto & Towing** <br> 9791 66th St. N. Pinellas Park <br> (727) 545-3596 | **ABC Towing & Recovery** <br> 4460 107th Circle N. Clearwater <br> (727) 536-1219 |
| **J&J Auto Body** <br> 4950 72nd Ave. N. Pinellas Park <br> (727) 522-2134 | **Eveland's Towing & Transport** <br> 12895 Automobile Blvd. Clearwater <br> (727) 536-8130 |
| **Frank's Body Shop** <br> 12405 49th St. N. Clearwater <br> (727) 573-2639 | **Florida Body Shop** <br> 6363 Ulmerton Rd. Largo <br> (727) 536-3505 |
| **Pinellas Auto Body & Service** <br> 2084 Range Rd. Clearwater <br> (727) 446-4051 | **Day's Collision Paint & Repair** <br> 975 Florida Ave. Palm Harbor <br> (727) 784-2445 |
| **Pfeifer Auto Services** <br> 1261 San Christopher Dr. Dunedin <br> (727) 736-2755 | **Keller's Body Shop** <br> 10716 64th Ave. N. Seminole <br> (727) 393-3188 |
| **Prestige Automotive Recovery** <br> 11440 66th Street N. Largo <br> (727) 546-3079 | **Bradford's Towing** <br> 1553 Savannah Ave. Tarpon Springs <br> (727) 938-5511 |
| **Joe's Towing & Recovery** <br> 6670 114th Ave. Largo <br> (727) 541-2695 | |

## FIRST Secure the "Impound Release Form"

Do not travel to the towing company and expect them to automatically release your vehicle. In order to retrieve your vehicle from an impound towing yard you will first need to secure an "Impound Release Form" from the police agency that arrested you for DUI.

## How to Secure the "Impound Release Form"

If you are the lawfully registered owner of the car or truck, it will be necessary for you to demonstrate proof of ownership in the form of the vehicle registration, bill of sale, lease agreement, title or auto liability insurance documents. You must also demonstrate proof of your identification. If you are not the registered owner of the vehicle you will need to secure a notarized "power of attorney" from the vehicle's owner which authorizes you to pick up the car from the impound lot.

## How Can I Get the "Impound Release Form" When My Documents Are In My Car?!?

Most of our clients keep their vehicle registration and insurance card in the glove box of their car. To compound matters, the key to their residence is typically located on the same key ring as their vehicle's ignition key. Unfortunately, upon your release from the Pinellas County Jail, all of these items will likely be in the custody and control of the towing company. To add insult to injury, under Florida law, the arresting officer was required to seize your driver's license if you had an unlawful breath alcohol level or you refused to submit to Intoxilyzer testing. In many cases, a driver's license may be the only state issued photo ID that the motorist possessed. So, if you are the registered owner of the vehicle, but lack these necessary credentials, what can you do to secure the all-important "Impound Release Form?"

 We recommend visiting the arresting law enforcement agency. Be certain to take with you any and all documents associated with your arrest. You should also possess the proper attitude. Calmly explain the dilemma you currently find yourself in. If you are polite and respectful, the police officer "may" work with you by accessing and printing your online booking photo from the jail records to confirm your identity. He can likewise retrieve your registration and vehicle

11

title information from "DAVID," which is Florida's electronic "Driver and Vehicle Information Database." Armed with this confirming information, many police officers are willing to then issue the "Impound Release Form." On other occasions, a disgruntled police officer may require you to make a round trip to the impound lot to secure and return with the vehicle's registration document.

## 2. Minimizing Your Social Media Exposure

While your criminal charge is pending, avoiding publicity after arrest is essential. You can achieve this by monitoring your behavior and statements. Anything you do or say could later be reported to the court and used as:

◉ Incriminating statements in an effort to convict you;

◉ An aggravating factor at sentencing in an effort to show your lack of remorse; and/or

◉ Evidence that while your case was pending, you continued to violate the law.

### Tell Your Story Only to Your Lawyer

When facing criminal charges, you should only speak about the facts of your case to your attorney. Statements given to your attorney are protected under the attorney-client privilege and can never be used against you. However, this privilege does not apply if you tell somebody else the same information. Even though you may fully trust your family and friends, any conversations between you and them are not privileged communications. As a result, your conversations with them are subject to being used against you in court. Making statements to family or friends could therefore place them in a delicate position and subject them to being called as a witness against you.

If you tell your story to a third party it could also end up in the local newspaper or appear in other forms of media. Hundreds of people are arrested each day. Just because you were arrested, doesn't mean your case will be the focus of a Tampa Bay Times article. To the contrary, the sheer number of Pinellas County arrests makes the job of sifting out news worthy stories a daunting task for newspaper reporters. The news media is therefore very dependent upon both anonymous and identified tipsters to bring an interesting recent arrest to their attention. Telling your story to someone other than your lawyer only invites trouble.

## Maintaining a Low Profile: Stay Away from the Internet

 Many users of Twitter, Facebook, online blogs, or other online social websites, mistakenly believe that such sites are private. However, state prosecutors have increasingly been using incriminating statements on these sites to help convict defendants or to seek an enhanced sentence after trial. There have been several cases where defendants have let their guard down and confessed online to committing a crime. Others have detailed their methods of initially avoiding arrest or posted pictures of the crime scene. These indiscretions led, of course, to easy convictions for the prosecutor.

## Search Warrants & Your Private or Restricted Internet Entries

Law enforcement officers are aggressively searching privately restricted areas of the internet for incriminating evidence through the use of a search warrant. Young adults are the most likely candidates to post such information online. Many teenagers have been caught posting pictures of underage drinking and illegal drug use. Users often believe that only their "invited" peers can view the information they have posted. However, law enforcement agencies have repeatedly proven this not to be the case.

Don't make your case worse by posting information about you or your pending criminal matter. This is an area of communication critical to avoiding publicity after arrest. You should resist sharing such information as it could greatly assist law enforcement and the Pinellas County State Attorney's Office in securing a conviction or a lengthier sentence. Remaining quiet about your case also affords your attorney greater latitude in explaining or mitigating your conduct to the Judge.

## We Routinely Counsel Our Clients on Ways to
## Avoid Post-Arrest Publicity

We will not only discuss the facts of your case and appropriate defenses, but also counsel you on steps to avoid publicity after your arrest.

### 3. Collecting Evidence

**Save Your Receipts** - Your receipts can provide helpful information in your case whether they show you had a lot or a little to drink. If you did not keep your receipts, take notes on the restaurants or bars you visited. You may be able to get the receipts from your credit card company or from the business itself.

**Tell Friends and Family to Save Voicemails and Text Messages -** Often an arrest affidavit will state that the law enforcement officer who pulled you over perceived your speech to be "slurred". A voicemail to a friend or family member can provide proof that your speech was normal.

**Check on Surveillance** - There may be video evidence out there that can help with your case. If the restaurant, bar, gas station, etc. has surveillance cameras it may help provide essential information such as timeframes, drinks purchased, your behavior, and your ability to walk.

**Take Notes** - Write down everything you can remember from the 24 hours leading up to your traffic stop by law enforcement.

**Witnesses** – Anyone you interacted with leading up to your arrest could have important information that will help in defending your case.

### 4. Schedule a Free Consultation with a Pinellas County Criminal Defense Attorney

Be prepared to ask the following questions:

- What are the attorney's qualifications, training, and experience in DUI law?

- Does the DUI defense attorney possess valuable insight obtained as the result of working as a state prosecutor?

- Does the attorney routinely handle DUI cases in the Pinellas County Court system?

- Has the attorney acquired certifications, recognition, or licensing associated with DUI prosecution?

- What is the attorney's reputation in the Pinellas County legal community?

- Has the attorney been called upon to teach, lecture, or instruct others on DUI Topics?

# Can I Drive After My DUI Arrest?

If your license was valid at the time of your arrest for DUI, the uniform traffic citation you received serves as your temporary driver's license.

At the bottom of this traffic citation it expressly states, "Unless ineligible, this citation shall serve as a temporary driver's license and will expire at midnight on the 10th day following the date of suspension."

If you have any reservations about your ability to drive, you should call our office and discuss the matter with a member of our criminal defense team before getting back behind the wheel of a car.

# Your 10 Day Deadline: Protecting Your Privilege to Drive

Following your DUI arrest, Florida law imposes a non-negotiable 10-day deadline on your ability to protect your privilege to drive.

**This Means 10 CALENDAR DAYS  - NOT 10 Business Days**

In most cases, taking no action during this initial 10-day period <u>will</u> subject you to a mandatory suspension of your driving privilege. For this reason, it is crucial that you schedule a prompt, free consultation with a qualified attorney prior to this 10-day deadline. During your consultation, the attorney will discuss with you the administrative driver's suspension, as well as, options that may exist in our effort to avoid <u>any</u> interruption in your ability to lawfully operate a motor vehicle.

Most of our clients charged with DUI are understandably concerned about the impact this will have on their driving privilege. You need to be aware that a DUI arrest could result in two different driver's license suspensions.

1.) **The "administrative" suspension** – In many DUI cases, law enforcement will take your driver's license at the time of your DUI arrest. This DHSMV "administrative" suspension is automatic, even though your case has not yet been heard in court. If your case involves a breath or blood result of .08 or higher, your driver's license was administratively suspended for a period of six months to one year depending on your prior record. If your case involves a refusal to submit to breath, urine or blood testing, your license was administratively suspended for a period of one year to eighteen months depending on your prior record.

2.) **The "court" suspension** – There are criminal court DUI penalties that require the judge to again suspend your driver's license in the event you are later convicted of the DUI charge. This second suspension is separate and apart from the earlier administrative suspension. The court suspension does not begin unless or until you are found guilty by the court. Because it is a separate suspension, the time you have spent on the administrative suspension of your license IS NOT credited towards the court suspension. The criminal court suspension can range from as little as six months to as long as a permanent or lifetime suspension, depending on your prior record and the facts of your case.

Some DUI cases involve a situation where a person blew into the machine and the breath result was under .08. The person then agreed to submit a urine sample, which was then sent to the medical examiner's office for testing. Under that specific scenario, Florida law does not impose any administrative driver's license suspension. (See the Chapter regarding Drugs, Urine and Blood testing.)

# Is a DHSMV Formal Administrative Review Hearing in My Best Interest?

One of the important decisions that an individual who has recently been arrested for a DUI must make is whether to have a DHSMV Formal Administrative Review Hearing or whether to waive his/her right to such a hearing. Florida law provides that the driver only has ten (10) calendar days (not ten business days) to make this decision.

 **A Bit of History** - Prior to July 1, 2013, an individual charged with a first-time DUI would only have one option: a Formal Administrative Review Hearing. Here's how it would work:

- If an individual who is arrested for a first DUI offense had a breath alcohol level that was over a .08, his/her driver's license would be suspended for a period of six (6) months.
- If he/she refused to submit to a breath test, his/her license would be suspended for a period of one (1) year.
- If the driver had a valid driver's license at the time of his/her arrest, the DUI citation serves as a full license to drive for ten (10) days. The driver must have the citation in the car with him/her when driving during that period of time.

The driver's attorney would file for a Formal Administrative Review Hearing on or before the tenth day after the driver's arrest.

When the attorney did so, the DHSMV would issue a "Temporary Driving Permit" that would allow the driver to continue driving for "Business Purposes Only" for an additional six (6) weeks.

During this time, a Formal Administrative Review Hearing would be conducted that would determine whether the driver would have his/her privilege to drive fully reinstated, or whether the suspension would stay on the driver's record.

If the attorney was successful in convincing the DHSMV to invalidate the suspension, the driver would be given a legal document that he/she could take to a regular tax collector's or driver's license office to obtain a driver's license.

If the attorney was unsuccessful at the DHSMV hearing, the driver would suffer a period of thirty (30) days during which he/she could not drive at all for any reason if the suspension was for having a breath alcohol level above .08. Thereafter, the driver could apply for a hardship license for the remainder of the six-month suspension, so long as he/she had enrolled in the DUI School.

If the suspension was for a refusal to submit to testing, the driver would suffer a period of ninety (90) days during which the driver could not drive at all for any reason. Thereafter, the driver could apply for a hardship license, so long as he/she had enrolled in DUI School.

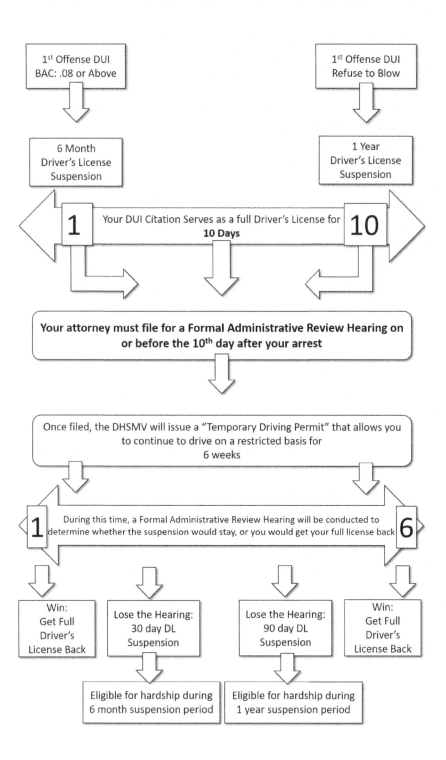

1st Offense DUI
BAC: .08 or Above

1st Offense DUI
Refuse to Blow

6 Month
Driver's License
Suspension

1 Year
Driver's License
Suspension

**1** Your DUI Citation Serves as a full Driver's License for
**10 Days** **10**

**Your attorney must file for a Formal Administrative Review Hearing on or before the 10th day after your arrest**

Once filed, the DHSMV will issue a "Temporary Driving Permit" that allows you to continue to drive on a restricted basis for
6 weeks

**1** During this time, a Formal Administrative Review Hearing will be conducted to determine whether the suspension would stay, or you would get your full license back **6**

Win:
Get Full
Driver's
License Back

Lose the Hearing:
30 day DL
Suspension

Lose the Hearing:
90 day DL
Suspension

Win:
Get Full
Driver's
License Back

Eligible for hardship during
6 month suspension period

Eligible for hardship during
1 year suspension period

## Waiver of the Formal Administrative Review Process:
## A New Option

On July 1, 2013, the legislature, probably for the only time in history, made the DUI law a little easier on persons who were charged with a first offense DUI. In that regard, Florida law was amended in such a way that a first-time DUI offender could exercise an option of "waiving" the formal administrative review process and secure a hardship license for the entire suspension. In other words, by waiving the right to challenge the suspension, the driver can avoid the "hard" suspension during which they could not drive at all.

To take advantage of the "waiver" option, an individual must do four things within the first 10 days:

**1.) Enroll in DUI School.**

**2.) Appear at the DHSMV Bureau of Administrative Reviews to request a hardship license through the "waiver" process.**

**3.) Go to a tax collector's office in order to obtain the hardship license.**

**4.) Bring the necessary documentation to the tax collector's office in order to become "Real ID Compliant" (if not previously verified).**

## Choosing Whether to Have a Formal Administrative Review Hearing or to Waive a Formal Administrative Review Hearing

For many of our clients, the opportunity to avoid a "hard suspension" by electing the "waiver process" is the best option. For those individuals, the inability to drive to work, school, or medical appointments for a period of 30 or 90 days would simply create too much of a hardship.

As with anything in life, accepting the suspension by waiving your right to a formal administrative review hearing has its disadvantages.

Listed below are some, but certainly not all, of the disadvantages of waiving your right to a Formal Administrative Review Hearing:

- If you waive your right to a Formal Administrative Review Hearing, you do not have a chance to win the hearing.

- If you waive your right to a Formal Administrative Review Hearing, a suspension will appear on your driving record for "Driving With an Unlawful Breath/Blood Alcohol Level" or "Refusal to Submit to Testing" even if the underlying DUI charge is later reduced to "Reckless Driving."

- Some insurance companies will interpret the administrative suspension for "Driving With an Unlawful Breath/Blood Alcohol Level" or "Refusal to Submit to Testing" as a sign that you are a high risk driver and raise or cancel your policy, even if your DUI charge is later reduced or dismissed.

- By waiving your right to a Formal Administrative Review Hearing, you give up the opportunity to have your attorney subpoena and cross-examine the law enforcement officers under oath at your DHSMV hearing. Because Rule 3.220 of the Florida Rules of Criminal Procedure prohibit an attorney from taking depositions in misdemeanor cases, the DHSMV hearing is often the only opportunity that your attorney will have to question law enforcement under oath, short of an evidentiary hearing or jury trial.

Our advice is simple: if you can stomach a period of 30 or 90 days during which you would not be able to drive, then common sense suggests that you should have a DHSMV Formal Administrative Review Hearing. It gives you an opportunity to keep the suspension off of your record, the chance to "win" your driver's license back, and, in some cases, gives your attorney the opportunity to uncover otherwise unavailable testimony and evidence that may help you with your pending criminal case.

If the inability to drive for 30 or 90 days would simply create too much of a hardship for you or your family, then perhaps a waiver of the Formal Administrative Review is in your best interest.

If you elect to "waive" your right to have a Formal Administrative Review Hearing, our office will provide you with a step-by-step guide instructing you how to apply for your hardship license. If you instead choose to challenge the administrative suspension by having a Formal Administrative Review hearing, our office will prepare all of the necessary paperwork during your initial consultation and hand deliver it on your behalf to the DHSMV Bureau of Administrative Reviews.

# How to Apply for a Hardship License

If it becomes necessary for you to obtain a hardship license, we can help you prepare so that you can easily and quickly navigate the application process.

We will advise you on your eligibility for a hardship license and inform you of the proper time to apply.

◉ Are you "Real ID" compliant? We can provide you with written instructions on what you need to do to satisfy this requirement of Florida and Federal Law.

◉ We can explain the difference between a "business purpose" and "employment purpose" hardship licenses as defined by Florida Statute Section 322.271.

◉ Our office can provide you with the necessary application forms and information packets to expedite your reinstatement efforts.

◉ We can counsel you, in advance, about the type and nature of questions the hearing officer may ask of you when determining whether to grant your reinstatement of driving privileges.

◉ We can provide you with specific "real-life" examples of past DHSMV Reinstatement Review Hearings to enable a comparison with the facts of your own case.

◉ We can provide you with advice and tips on the proper use of a hardship license in order to help you avoid a potential new criminal charge of Driving on a Suspended License or Violation of Your Driver's License Restriction.

### You May Have Only One Opportunity to Get it Right

For the most part, you only get one opportunity to state your case during the hardship license application process at the DHSMV. The denial of a hardship license caused by your inexperience or the volunteering of what you thought were innocent admissions, can be a costly mistake. When you attend the free consultation at our office, we can discuss the individual facts of your case that support your contention that your inability to lawfully operate a motor vehicle will result in a hardship to you or your family.

### DUI Arrest for a CDL License Holder
### Your License is Your Livelihood

 If you were recently arrested for a DUI Offense, and are the holder of a commercial driver's license (CDL), you already know that there are serious consequences to your continued employment and livelihood.

The options available to a CDL holder are significantly less than those drivers who simply have a Class E driver's license. For example, although a CDL holder may exercise the "waiver" option to obtain a hardship license following a DUI arrest, the hardship license does not permit the driver to operate commercial vehicles. Thus, if a CDL holder wants to be able to maintain driving commercial vehicles, his attorney must file a Request for a Formal Administrative Review Hearing.

Florida Statute Section 322.61 provides for certain disqualifications of a CDL after an alcohol-related arrest or conviction.

A one-year disqualification applies to any of the following circumstances:

◉ Driving a commercial motor vehicle with a blood alcohol level (BAC) of .04 or above;

- A conviction for driving a motor vehicle while under the influence of alcohol or a controlled substance;

- A suspension for refusal to submit to a breath test to determine the alcohol concentration while operating or in actual physical control of a commercial motor vehicle;

- A conviction for driving a commercial motor vehicle while under the influence of alcohol or controlled substance;

- A conviction for driving a commercial motor vehicle while in possession of a controlled substance.

An arrest or conviction for any of the above-mentioned scenarios will result in a revocation of your CDL for a period of one year. Of course, in addition to the CDL revocation, all of the other court penalties and a suspension to your regular driver's license discussed earlier would also apply.

Second or subsequent arrests or convictions for the above-referenced situations can result in a permanent disqualification from driving a commercial motor vehicle. Furthermore, Florida law does not provide for any hardship, business purpose only, or employment purpose only driver's license to operate a commercial motor vehicle. The disqualification acts as a ban on driving a commercial vehicle for any reason during the entire period of disqualification.

Given the tremendous ramifications that a DUI conviction may have on the livelihood of a Florida CDL driver, it is of the utmost importance that he or she retain the services of a highly-experienced DUI defense team to challenge the arrest.

In some cases, law enforcement will make errors that only pertain to CDL drivers that may benefit our client's cases. For example, if an officer advised you of the consequences of refusing a breath test as it relates to a regular Class E driver's license, but did not advise you of the consequences of your refusal as it applied to your CDL, you may be entitled to have the suspension for refusal to submit to testing invalidated.

# Your First Court Date – the "Arraignment"

The first court date in any criminal case is called an Arraignment. If you were arrested for a misdemeanor DUI offense, your arrest affidavit and citation should reflect an "Arraignment" date. This legal proceeding will be scheduled at either the North County Traffic Court facility or the South County Traffic Court facility. The purpose of an Arraignment is to formally advise you of the charge pending against you and to allow you to enter a plea of Not Guilty, Guilty, or No Contest.

It is important to understand that the arraignment is <u>not</u> a trial. At the arraignment hearing, the Judge does not have the authority to dismiss your case, reduce the charge, or find you "Not Guilty." If you have not hired an attorney, your attendance at the court date scheduled for your arraignment is <u>mandatory</u>. Your failure to attend this hearing will likely result in the judge issuing a "failure to appear" warrant for your arrest.

However, if you timely retain the services of an attorney to represent you on your DUI charge, your lawyer may excuse your presence at the arraignment hearing. In most cases your attorney will file a written plea of "Not Guilty" with the Clerk of Court. This will have the effect of removing your arraignment hearing from the court docket.

In some limited circumstances, our office will request that you accompany your lawyer to the arraignment hearing. Sometimes, as a condition of release from the Pinellas County Jail, the Judge may order an individual to wear an alcohol monitoring ankle bracelet. If an ankle bracelet requirement was imposed in your case, we may determine that it is appropriate to attend the arraignment hearing. We can use this hearing to request permission from the Judge to remove your alcohol ankle monitoring device.

If you were arrested for a Felony DUI, DUI with Serious Bodily Injury, or DUI Manslaughter, you will likely not have a court date listed on your criminal arrest affidavit or citation(s). The reason for this is that the State Attorney's Office will conduct its own independent investigation into the facts and circumstances of your case to determine whether the formal filing of a criminal charge is appropriate. If the State files an "Information" officially charging you with a Felony DUI offense, the Clerk of Court will mail you notice of your arraignment date.

### Subsequent Court Hearings – Pre-Trial Conferences

 If a person enters a plea of "Not Guilty" at the arraignment, the Judge will set a new court date called a "Pre-Trial Conference." The purpose of a subsequent "Pre-Trial" court hearing is for the Judge to inquire of the State and the defense as to the present status of the case and the efforts thus far to move the criminal charge towards resolution. Common issues that are often addressed at the Pre-Trial Conference may include the following:

◉ Is a continuance necessary because more time is needed to gather evidence, interview witnesses, obtain documents or review items that your attorney has acquired from the prosecutor?

◉ Has you attorney identified a legal issue in your case that requires an Evidentiary Motion Hearing before the case can go any further?

◉ Has an agreement been reached by the parties such that a plea bargain or negotiated resolution can be presented to the Judge?

◉ Whether the case must be scheduled for trial because the client finds the proposed plea bargain terms unacceptable.

DUI cases typically last four to eight months. During this litigation, there may be several Pre-Trial Conferences scheduled in the case. You will receive notice in advance from the Clerk of Court for each Pre-Trial Conference. Your lawyer will advise you as to whether your appearance at a Pre-Trial Conference can be excused.

Our office recognizes that your attendance at court proceedings may cause a hardship due to employment obligations, child care needs and/or your limited ability to drive. For these reasons, we make every effort to limit the number of court appearances that our client will be required to attend. This can often be accomplished by having our client sign a "Waiver of Appearance" authorizing our law firm to appear in court on your behalf.

# Resolving Your DUI Case Quickly vs. Seeking the Best Possible Outcome

The most important goal in your DUI case should be getting the *right result* and not the *quickest result*. A DUI charge is among the most complicated cases litigated within our criminal justice system. It often involves a review of the facts, anticipated "opinion" testimony and scientific evidence in the form of breath test, urine test, or blood test results. Legal issues are similarly multi-faceted because there are constitutional considerations, statutory requirements, and administrative regulations that need to be thoroughly analyzed and addressed.

We counsel our clients to productively use the time between the date of their arrest and the time their case is ultimately concluded. Their proactive efforts can often assist us in securing the best possible outcome. Some examples of this may include reinstating driver license privileges, completing DUI school, obtaining an alcohol or substance abuse evaluation, and completing any recommended counseling or treatment. In some cases, we may suggest that our clients perform some community service hours. The completion of these tasks can often make our client look better in the eyes of the Judge.

Our client's positive attitude can also be persuasive in the event that we enter into plea bargain negotiations with the State Attorney's Office.

You should know that performing these tasks in advance of your case being resolved, is not an admission of guilt. To the contrary, your proactive attitude may be part of our argument that you are deserving of a reduction of the charge from DUI to Reckless Driving. (See: Reduction to Reckless Driving Chapter for more information.)

# Evaluating Your DUI Case

Most DUI cases are founded on three key pieces of evidence:

**1.) Chemical Testing (Breath, Urine, or Blood)**

**2.) Field Sobriety Tests**

**3.) Police Reports**

# The Breath Test

Many clients conclude that if their breath test was above a .08 that "all is lost" and their case may not be worth fighting. However, a proper review of the breath testing procedures at the time of your arrest may cast a different light on your case.

The results of a breath test can sometimes be challenged in court and excluded from consideration. For instance, the Intoxilyzer results may be inaccurate or unreliable due to improper maintenance, calibration, or a lapse in certification for the machine or the operator's permit. Inaccurate Intoxilyzer readings could be caused by such things as burping or belching, the failure of law enforcement to properly observe you for a 20-minute period prior to breath testing, or the lack of proper training and continuing education on the part of the breath test operator.

In other cases, the breath test may not be admissible if your decision to submit a breath sample was coerced or made under duress. Florida law requires a showing that your decision to submit a breath sample into the Intoxilyzer machine was made freely and voluntarily before the results can be admissible in court.

Our office can secure the documents associated with the Intoxilyzer machine used in your case for a thorough evaluation that will determine whether all administrative rules and state statutes were complied with. Any substantial deviation from the correct procedures set forth in Florida law may provide a sufficient basis to have your breath test results thrown out. Depriving the prosecutor of this key piece of evidence could significantly strengthen our negotiating position.

## Law Enforcement's Burden

 Florida law places a burden on a driver to provide a breath test sample once arrested for DUI or suffer a potential administrative driver license suspension. However, a responsibility is also placed upon law enforcement to comply with many rules and regulations associated with the inspection, calibration, operation, and certification of the Intoxilyzer and those persons assigned to its care and use.

Our office is very familiar with the various nuances in the law associated with Intoxilyzer breath testing. Through our discovery process we will investigate whether the breath testing procedures in your case were consistent with the laws that govern the admissibility of the breath test results in court.

## The Prosecutor's Burden – 8 Critical Questions

**1.) Was the Intoxilyzer machine used in your case properly registered and approved for use by FDLE?** Florida Administrative Code 11D-8.003(2) requires that every Intoxilyzer machine used for law enforcement evidentiary purposes in the State of Florida be registered and approved by the Florida Department of Law Enforcement (FDLE.) In order to demonstrate compliance with this provision, the Prosecutor must produce a valid FDLE Registration Certificate corresponding to the specific machine used in your case.

**2.) Can the State produce proper documentation to show that a calibration check was performed in the month in which your test was administered?** Florida Administrative Code 11D-8.006(1) requires that a Police Agency's Inspector must perform specific regulatory inspections on all evidentiary breath testing machines at least once every calendar month.

**3.) Can the State produce proper documentation to show that an annual calibration check was performed on the Intoxilyzer machine used in your case?** Florida Administrative Code 11D-8.004(3) requires that all evidentiary breath testing machines be inspected by a Regional Alcohol Breath Testing Inspector employed by the Florida Department of Law Enforcement once each calendar year.

**4.) Was the Agency Inspector properly licensed in compliance with Florida Administrative Code 11D-8.002(5) and 11D-8.008(2) to perform calibration checks as evidenced by their FDLE Permitting Certificate?** If the Agency Inspector was properly licensed, had his/ her permit lapsed beyond the four-year period specified by Florida Administrative Code 11D-8.008(3)?

**5.) During law enforcement's calibration checks, did the Agency Inspector properly test the range of the Intoxilyzer's accuracy?** Florida Administrative Code 11D-8.002(1) requires minimum calibration testing by law enforcement of multiple tests, at three known alcohol concentration levels.

**6.) During FDLE's annual calibration check, did the Department Inspector properly test the range of the Intoxilyzer's accuracy?** Florida Administrative Code 11D-8.004(2) requires minimum calibration testing by FDLE of ten tests, at three known alcohol concentration levels.

**7.) Did the calibration checks performed by both the Agency Inspector and the FDLE Department Inspector reveal test results that fell outside of permitted deviation ranges?** Florida Administrative Code 11D-8.002(1) requires that the calibration checks result in a machine falling within the following acceptable ranges:
For a known .05 alcohol concentration the range is .045 – .055
For a known .08 alcohol concentration the range is .075 – .085
For a known .20 alcohol concentration the range is .190 – .210

**8.) Was the Intoxilyzer Operator in your case properly licensed in compliance with Florida Statutes Chapters 316, 322, 327 and Florida Administrative Code 11D-8.002(17) to lawfully conduct breath testing?** If the Intoxilyzer Operator was properly licensed, had his/her permit lapsed beyond the four-year period specified by Florida Administrative Code 11D-8.008(3)?

## How Important is the Calibration Procedure?

Our office retained the services of local Patent and Trademark attorney, Anton Hopen, who secured for us copies of the various patents issued to CMI, Inc. This company is the manufacturer of the Intoxilyzer breath testing machines used by law enforcement throughout Pinellas County. Our review of these patents revealed a concession on the part of the manufacturer that even minor deviations in the proper calibration of the machine can result in major inaccuracies during the breath testing procedure. Reproduced below is the exact language used by the manufacturer to express their clear concern for any machine that has not been subject to timely calibration and maintenance.

United States Patent and Trademark Office
Patent Number: 5,422,485
Application Filed: July 9, 1993
Issue Date of Patent: June 6, 1995
Inventor: Harvey F. Bowlds Assignee: CMI, Inc.

"Precise and reliable calibration of infrared breath alcohol measuring instruments is very important because even small errors in the measured attenuation can cause relatively large errors in the alcohol content determined by the computer. To avoid improper arrest and charges, including for driving under-the-influence, and to maintain the credibility of the instruments and alcohol readings taken thereby, reliable and precise calibration is required."

*— Excerpt from the Patent Specification, Background of the Invention Section, Column 1, Lines 44-60*

## What if a Calibration or Maintenance Problem is Discovered in Your Case?

Florida Statute Section 316.194(3) provides that the prosecutor may introduce breath test results <u>only</u> upon a showing of "substantial compliance" with the administrative rules. If your attorney can point to a failure on the part of law enforcement to comply with the many administrative rules, statutes and other requirements, the Court then has the authority and obligation to prevent the prosecutor from introducing your breath test results in court.

Having your breath test results excluded will often place you in a superior negotiating position that could result in a reduction of the charge to a "Reckless Driving" offense. In some cases, the suppression of the breath test readings may result in an outright dismissal of the DUI charge.

# The Blood Test

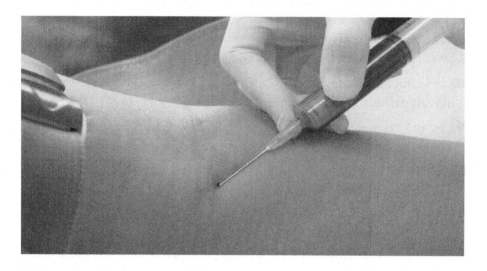

Florida Law only permits the taking of a blood sample under limited circumstances in DUI cases. Both the Florida legislature and the Florida courts have restricted the taking of blood because of the invasive nature of the procedure. Currently, there are three common scenarios where blood evidence will be a part of the DUI Case:

◉ Voluntary consent to a blood draw

◉ A search warrant permitting a blood draw

◉ A blood draw accomplished at the hospital pursuant to the provisions of Florida's "Implied Consent" scheme

## Voluntary Blood Draw

The results of a blood test may be admissible in court if there is a finding that the defendant "voluntarily consented" to the blood draw. However, there are many factors that the court must consider that may cause a blood draw to be deemed "involuntary." For example, courts in Florida have found consent to be involuntary when:

- Law enforcement advised the defendant that he would lose his license if he did not provide a blood sample;

- Law enforcement advised the defendant that he would be arrested if he did not provide a blood sample;

- Law enforcement suggested that the penalties or punishments would be less if the defendant agreed to provide a blood sample; or

- The defendant was not advised that the blood draw was being conducted voluntarily and that Florida's Implied Consent law only required submission to a breath or urine test.

Thus, if your case involves a blood draw, your DUI Defense Team must conduct a careful analysis to determine if the blood draw was truly "voluntary." A finding that the blood draw was involuntary may result in the exclusion or suppression of the blood evidence in court.

## Appearance at a Hospital and Taking of Breath/Urine was Impractical or Impossible

Florida Statute Section 316.1932(c) provides that, in scenarios where the taking of breath or urine is impractical or impossible, law enforcement may, instead, request that a subject submit to blood testing for the purpose of alcohol content analysis. Moreover, it provides that if a subject is unconscious and incapable of refusing, he is presumed to have consented to the test.

If a blood draw is obtained through this provision of Florida Law, your DUI Defense Team must carefully analyze each factor that the prosecutor must prove in order to demonstrate that law enforcement substantially complied with the requirements of this statute.

For example:

- Did the client appear at a medical facility?

- Was it truly impractical to obtain a breath test or was the treatment brief in nature?

- In the case of a "drug" or prescription medication DUI, was it impractical or impossible to obtain a urine sample at the medical facility?

- Did law enforcement ever inquire of medical personnel how long the defendant was expected to be in the hospital?

### Challenging the Admissibility of Your Blood Test Results

 Blood test results collected through Florida's "Implied Consent" statutes must be obtained through procedures that comply with Florida's Administrative Rules governing blood testing, found in Florida Administrative Code Chapter 11D-8. It is imperative that a qualified and experienced DUI Defense attorney carefully examine the existence and compliance of the following blood test documents. Defect or omission can be grounds for the exclusion of your blood tests results in court.

- Request for Toxicological Analysis: This form is used to establish chain of custody between law enforcement and the medical examiner's office.

- Certification of Blood Withdrawal: This form is required by the Florida Administrative Code, FDLE/ATP - Form 11. The State Attorney's Office will need this document to demonstrate that the person who performed the blood draw was a person authorized to do so by Florida Law. Likewise, the State will need this document to establish that the proper blood draw procedure (outlined by F.A.C. 11D-8.012) was used by the person who completed the draw.

- Blood Alcohol Analysis Affidavit: This form is required by the Florida Administrative Code, FDLE/ATP - Form 15. It records the blood test results that were obtained from the Defendant's blood sample.

- Results of Laboratory Analysis: This document reports the blood test results and is generated by the Pinellas County Forensic Laboratory. This official document must reflect that the blood draw collection tubes were coated with an approved anticoagulant as required by F.A.C. 11D-8.012(2).

Florida's administrative code 11D-8.012(4) likewise requires an entry on the document that accurately reflects the date and time of the blood draw as reported on the collection tubes.

- ◉ Blood Alcohol Analyst Permit: This evidence of licensure is needed to demonstrate that the person who utilized the gas chromatograph mass spectrometer was properly trained and qualified to conduct evidentiary blood alcohol testing. F.A.C. 11D-8.013 provides a list of the qualifications necessary to obtain a Blood Alcohol Analysis Permit from the Florida Department of Law Enforcement.

- ◉ Blood Collection Tube Labels: The blood collection tube labels are required under F.A.C. 11D-8.012(4) to include the name of the person tested, date and time sample was collected, and initials of person who collected the sample.

- ◉ Blood Kit Box: Although not specifically required by the Florida Administrative Code, your DUI Defense Team will request photographs of the blood collection kit. A review of these photographs may reveal that the blood kit's contents was incomplete, damaged or otherwise tampered with. Likewise, a review of these photographs is necessary because the exterior of the kit provides the Expiration Date and Lot Number of the blood collection tubes.

### Other Methods of Obtaining Blood Test Results

Florida Statute Section 316.1933(2)(a)(1) provides that medical personnel are permitted to inform law enforcement if an individual has a blood alcohol level that is .08 or above.

If a blood draw was performed by a hospital or treatment provider for medical purposes, the State Attorney's Office could later issue a subpoena for your medical records. In order to legally do so, the State Attorney's Office must provide you with written notice of its intention to issue a subpoena for medical records that are otherwise confidential. Upon receipt of this notice, we have ten days to file a written objection to the issuance of the subpoena. Thereafter, the burden is on the State Attorney's Office to schedule a hearing so that the Court can determine whether the subpoena is proper, seeks evidence that is relevant to the case, and limited in scope so as to not infringe upon your otherwise confidential medical records.

# Constitutional Protections that Could Cause Your Blood Alcohol Results to be Inadmissible in Court

 The Fourth Amendment provides in relevant part that "[t]he right of the people to be secure in their persons, houses, papers, and effects, against unreasonable searches and seizures, shall not be violated, and no Warrants shall issue, but upon probable cause." Both Florida cases and Federal cases have held that a warrantless search of the person is reasonable only if it falls within a recognized exception. See, e.g., *United States v. Robinson*, 414 U.S. 218, 224 (1973).

That same principle applies to blood draws. A blood draw is a compelled physical intrusion into a person's veins to obtain a sample of blood for use as evidence against them in a criminal investigation. Such an invasion of bodily integrity implicates an individual's "most personal and deep-rooted expectations of privacy." *Winston v. Lee*, 470 U.S. 753, 760 (1985).

In the recent Supreme Court case of *Missouri v. McNeely*, 133 S.Ct. 1552 (2013) the Court considered whether a warrantless blood draw was lawful. "Exigent circumstances" are a well-known exception to Fourth Amendment protection. In *McNeely*, the Supreme Court held that the fact that alcohol in one's blood dissipates over time is not, in itself, a *per se* exigent circumstance (though, the Court stated, in dicta, that there may be cases where the elimination of alcohol over time may create an exigent circumstance). The Court also noted that states may provide an individual with greater constitutional protections, but they cannot limit one's constitutional protections.

The United States Supreme Court expanded on the *McNeely* decision in 2016, in the case of *Birchfield v. N. Dakota*, 579 U. S. _____ (2016), the Supreme Court held that the administration of a blood test to determine blood alcohol content, without first obtaining a warrant, violates an individual's Fourth Amendment protection from unreasonable search and seizure. The Court reasoned that, due to the invasiveness of the test and the privacy concerns of the government possessing a sample of an individual's blood, there would be no justification in requiring a blood test when the much less invasive breath test was available.

Absent particular "exigent circumstances," blood tests may not be administered on a defendant without consent, unless law enforcement first obtains a warrant. Furthermore, the Court held that individuals cannot be "compelled" to consent to a blood test by the threat that a refusal would be a criminal act unto itself. The Court found that it was not reasonable that a motorist must "impliedly consent" to submit to a blood test on pain of committing a criminal offense merely through exercising the privilege of using public roadways.

As a result, an argument may exist that, although the State complied with Florida's Implied Consent statute, the law, as a whole, is unconstitutional and is contrary to the ruling in the landmark *McNeely* and *Birchfield* cases.

# The Urine Test

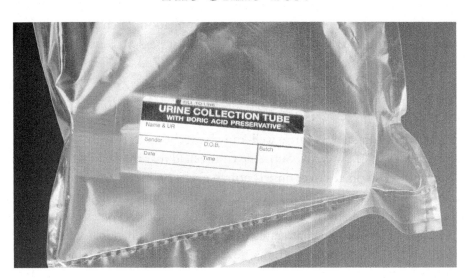

In some DUI cases, the law enforcement officer may suspect that you were impaired by drugs or prescription medication, rather than by alcoholic beverages. Therefore, a urine test may be sought instead of, or in addition to, a breath test. Florida Statute Section 316.1932(1)(b) provides that law enforcement may lawfully request a urine sample if a defendant has been arrested for driving under the influence of chemical or controlled substances. There are a number of factual, legal, and scientific issues associated with the so-called "drugged driving case." We explore all of these defenses later in this book.

# What if I Refused the Breath, Blood or Urine Test?

If you refused the breath test, blood test, or a urine test, the State Attorney's Office will lack direct evidence of your impairment, but they will use your refusal to argue your "consciousness of guilt." Your attorney may be able to present reasonable explanations as to why you refused to submit to a breath, blood, or urine test and can emphasize that the State lacks precise physical evidence to demonstrate your impairment.

As a result, when deciding whether to submit to a breath and/or blood or urine test, you must weigh the consequences of a refusal against the danger of arming the State with evidence that you may have had a test result over the legal limit.

Our experience has shown that those DUI cases that are reduced to a "Reckless Driving" tend to be those where the State doesn't have breath, blood, or urine test evidence on its side and where our client does not looked impaired on the video recorded Field Sobriety Tests.

# Roadside Field Sobriety Tests and Your DUI Video

Most DUI cases that arise out of Pinellas County entail police administering Field Sobriety Tests to determine if you should be arrested.

Commons examples include:

◙ walk and turn test,

◙ finger to nose test,

◙ one leg stand test, and

◙ the administration of the horizontal gaze nystagmus test.

 These tests are typically recorded on video and are used to assist the officer in his determination if an arrest for DUI is appropriate. The officer's interpretation of your performance on these roadside tests may be challenged based on a variety of reasons. These include such considerations as whether you suffer from a physical, mental, or medical problem that would have impacted your performance.

Likewise, it may be important to learn if you were nervous, tired, or distracted during the testing procedures. Moreover, our careful review of the video itself is critical. For example, the video may have limited utility in court due to a lack of audio or poor video quality. The footage might be of limited evidentiary value where a review reveals that your performance may have been affected by traffic, noise, or poor lighting conditions. In some cases, we find that our client's performance on video is inconsistent with the description provided in the police officer's narrative offense report.

## We Can Secure a Copy of Your DUI Video

 Our office will secure a copy of the video taken at the time of your arrest. It is our practice to subject these videos to close scrutiny in order to determine whether the Field Sobriety Tests were properly explained and demonstrated in accordance with the standards of the National Highway and Traffic Safety Administration. Further, a review of your video will provide us with a better understanding of your appearance, your speech, and your overall demeanor at the time of your traffic stop. Your appearance on video may provide us with the ammunition to negotiate a reduction of the DUI charge in your case to the lesser offense of Reckless Driving.

# Scrutinizing the Police Reports

COMPLAINT/ARREST AFFIDAVIT – CIRCUIT/COUNTY COURT – PINELLAS COUNTY, FLORIDA

| OBTS # | | REPORT # | | DOCKET # | |
|---|---|---|---|---|---|
| Person ID | | | SSN# | | |
| Charge Description ☐Felony ☐Misdemeanor ☐Warrant ☐Traffic ☐Ordinance | | Traffic Citation # (if any) | | Court Case # | |
| Charge | | | | | |

| Defendant's Name (Last, First, Middle) | DOB | Sex | Race | Ht | Wt | Hair | Eyes | Skin |
|---|---|---|---|---|---|---|---|---|
| Alias | DL # | State | Scars/Marks/Tattoos/Physical Features | | | | | |
| Local Address (Street, City, State, Zip Code) | Telephone | Place of Birth | Citizenship | | | | | |
| Permanent Address (Street, City, State, Zip Code) | Telephone | Employed by / School | | | | | | |

| Weapon Seized  Type ☐Yes   ☐No | Indication of  Y  N  UNK Drug Influence ☐ ☐ ☐ | Indication of Mental Y  N  UNK Health Issues       ☐ ☐ ☐ | Indication of         Y  N  UNK Alcohol Influence ☐ ☐ ☐ |
|---|---|---|---|
| Co-Defendant's Name (Last, First, Middle) | DOB | Sex  Race | In Custody ☐Yes ☐No ☐Felony ☐Misdemeanor |
| Co-Defendant's Name (Last, First, Middle) | DOB | Sex  Race | In Custody ☐Yes ☐No ☐Felony ☐Misdemeanor |

The undersigned swears that he/she has reasonable grounds to believe that the above named defendant on the _____ day of_____ . _____

The criminal arrest affidavit you may have received at the Pinellas County Jail is commonly referred to as a "booking advisory." Contrary to popular belief, this document is not the police report. Rather, it only contains the bare facts sufficient to establish probable cause for the purpose of effectuating your arrest. A full and complete narrative police report is generated by the officer after your arrest. This narrative account begins with your driving pattern, describes your field sobriety testing and discusses any other facts and circumstances leading up to and including your ultimate arrest. The police report also documents statements or admissions you may have made, and includes a variety of other observations related to your state of sobriety.

It must be remembered that the police report is only the officer's "opinion" or "subjective interpretation" of the events leading up to your arrest. Our office can secure a copy of the full narrative police report in your case and carefully review it with you. We will be able to examine the facts recounted within the report and compare the officer's account with what we observe on the video. We can also compare the report with your own recollection of events, along with the observations of any passengers in your vehicle. Further, we will be able to determine if the initial basis for stopping your motor vehicle is one that was legally justified under the law. Our review of the police report may uncover violations of your constitutional rights that may result in the exclusion of incriminating statements or other critical evidence in your case.

# Illegal Drugs and Prescription Medications

Many people are surprised to learn that they can be arrested for DUI even though they consumed little or no alcohol. In fact, Florida Law permits a DUI arrest where the officer has probable cause to believe you are impaired by alcohol or a "controlled substance." This includes illegal drugs such as marijuana and opioids as well as prescription medication.

### A Valid Prescription Written by Your Doctor is Not a Defense to DUI

One common misconception that is widely held by the public is that having a valid prescription for a medication is a defense to DUI This is simply not true. Having a prescription for a medication only allows you to own, use, or possess the medication. It does not give you the right to drive after having consumed the medication, if taking the prescription drug causes you to be impaired while driving. Thus, a DUI prosecution can be premised on impairment by either alcohol, illegal drugs, prescription medications or any combination thereof. However, you will later learn that prosecutions premised on impairment caused by illegal drugs or prescription medications can be more difficult for the State to prove than a straight forward alcohol related DUI case.

By far, the most common law enforcement investigative technique in drug or prescription medication related DUI offenses is urine testing. However, the use of urinalysis evidence in a DUI case is subject to many constraints and shortcomings.

# The Limitations of Urine Testing in DUI Drug Related Cases

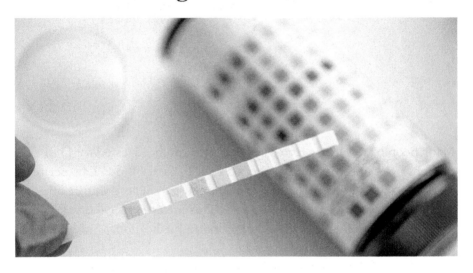

While a urine sample may reveal the presence of a prescription medication or illegal drug, the mere presence of either is **not enough** by itself to suggest impairment at the time of driving.

Ron Bell, former Chief Toxicologist for the Pinellas County Forensic Laboratory, regularly explains the limitations of urinalysis in the following fashion:

*"A urine drug screen takes place in a laboratory setting and involves multiple chemists and technicians. The process entails a battery of tests over the course of several days utilizing different instruments that represent a comprehensive examination for controlled substances. These tests include the 'immunoassay presumptive test,' the 'thin layer chromatography test,' the 'gas chromatography test' and 'mass spectrometry.' Some of these tests are 'quantitative' which reveal concentration levels. However, in a urine test, the results are always reported in a 'qualitative' fashion. <u>Meaning that the results are reported in such a way that they are limited only to confirm the presence or absence of a drug</u>."*

Simply confirming the presence or absence of a drug in urinalysis testing is premised on the scientific affirmation that drug concentrations detected in urine do not correlate with concentrations found in the blood. Thus, urine concentration levels have no meaning in and of themselves since they represent a number related to what is found merely in the urine and not in the blood stream. And of course, it is only what is found in the blood stream that directly relates to the ultimate determination of impairment at the time of driving.

It is interesting to note that the only time a toxicologist might be able to provide expert testimony as to whether a driver might have felt the effects of the drug at the time of his/her driving, is if there was precise reliable information available concerning the dosage and the time the driver either ingested or inhaled the drug. Thus, urine testing, by its very nature is imprecise and difficult to interpret.

Usually, the State's toxicologist can only testify that while the presence of a controlled substance may have been detected in the urine sample, it is impossible to determine whether the driver was actually feeling the effects of that substance at the time he/she was operating the vehicle. Typically, the toxicologist will have to admit that such uncertainty is due to the length of time that it takes for most drugs to be processed or "eliminated" into the urine by the human body.

### How Long Can Drugs Remain Detectable in the Urine?

Most drugs can remain in the human body for some time. For instance, THC, tetrahydrocannabinol, is a by-product of marijuana metabolism in the body. With just one smoke, it can be detected in a urine sample for up to 3-5 days. The moderate use of marijuana, for example 3 times per week, can be detected for 8-12 days. Daily marijuana use will test positive in the urine for 21-30+ days. The chart below reveals the testing limitations of other drugs and prescription medications.

| | |
|---|---|
| Heroin/Morphine | 1 - 3 days (possible only one day) |
| Methadone | 1 - 2 days (very dose dependent) |
| Dihydrocodeine | 4 - 5 days (in high concentration) |
| Codeine | 2 - 3 days |
| Pholcodeine | 10 - 15 days |
| Amphetamines | 1 - 2 days (can be detected up to 4 days) |
| Cocaine | 12 hrs - 3 days |
| Benzodiazepines | 1 day - 3 weeks (acute v. chronic use) |
| Barbiturates | days - weeks (dependant on type) |
| Ecstasy | 2 - 4 days |
| Temgesic | 2 - 3 days |
| Alcohol | 12 - 24 hours |

## Urinalysis vs. Blood Draw

Urinalysis is a far inferior method of testing when compared to a drug screen conducted with a **blood draw**. Blood analysis can provide much more accurate evidence of what substances (and in what concentration) were actually in the driver's **blood stream** at the time law enforcement was conducting their DUI investigation. We discussed previously, the legal issues associated with the restrictions that Florida law places on blood draws in DUI cases.

## Did the Police Ask for Both Breath and Urine Testing in Your DUI Case?

If an arrested driver submits to Intoxilyzer breath testing that returns results under the legal limit of .08 it is common practice for law enforcement to then request a urine sample. This form of double testing is permitted under Florida's Implied Consent law which authorizes law enforcement to request **both** a breath sample to determine the presence of alcohol and a urine sample to determine the presence of drugs. However, law enforcement must have a good faith belief that a driver is impaired by prescription medication or illegal drugs to request the urine sample. We often find that law enforcement simply requests a urine sample automatically after a person blows under the legal limit. Under those circumstances the request for a urine sample may be unlawful and the results or your refusal to provide urine may be excluded from evidence.

## A Urinalysis Case May be a Good Candidate for Reduction to the Lesser Offense of Reckless Driving

Because urinalysis results are of questionable value in demonstrating that a person was under the influence of an illegal drug or prescription medication <u>at the time of driving</u>, these cases are sometimes viewed as good candidates for a reduction to a Reckless Driving charge. Such a determination is obviously dependent on a review of the video evidence and other potential mitigating factors in the case. An experienced attorney can sometimes intervene on a client's behalf and point out these weaknesses in the prosecutor's case. Such intervention may convince the prosecutor assigned to the case that he may be unlikely to prevail at trial and that it would be in the best interests of both parties to reduce the DUI charge.

## How Our Office Can Help

 The lawyers in our office have over 20 years of combined experience in handling these unique DUI cases. We have studied the scientific and evidentiary issues involved in drug / medication related DUI cases. We also understand the strengths and weaknesses that flow from the use of this evidence in court. We can evaluate all the facts and circumstances of your case, including whether law enforcement employed the services of a certified "drug recognition expert." Such a review is critical to advising you on the best possible course of action, including whether your case may be a good candidate for reduction to Reckless Driving.

# Other Possible Defenses

Depending on the specific facts of your case, you may have a number of potential defenses. An experienced attorney can review your situation and may be able to challenge several aspects of the prosecution's case, including:

◙ Did the officer have probable cause to believe that you committed a traffic infraction that would allow him to initiate a vehicle traffic stop and detain you in the first place?

◙ If the officer did not observe a traffic infraction, did the officer have a reasonable articulable suspicion of criminal activity that allowed him to initiate a vehicle traffic stop and detain you in the first place?

◙ The law enforcement officer must have "reasonable suspicion" under the law to stop your vehicle. He cannot stop you based on a mere hunch that you may be impaired. Without a lawful justification for the stop, all of the evidence obtained thereafter is in jeopardy of being excluded from the subsequent court proceedings.

◙ Whether you were in fact the driver of the vehicle or actually "operating" the vehicle. In some cases, there may not be a witness available to the State that can "put you behind the wheel."

◙ Were the field sobriety tests administered properly and were the results reported accurately? An in-depth analysis of the video by our office could reveal inaccuracies or errors in the officer's DUI investigation.

◙ After the arrest, did the officer read you your Miranda warnings? If he failed to do so, we may be able to exclude damaging statements made after the arrest.

◉ Could your case benefit from the "Rising Blood Alcohol Defense?" When you drink an alcoholic beverage, the alcohol will continue to be absorbed into your body. Typically, it can take over an hour between the time you are stopped by law enforcement and the time you submit a breath sample at the police station. In that hour, depending on when you had your last drink, your blood alcohol content (BAC) could keep rising and the results of your test will show a higher BAC than when you were driving. This is a potential problem for the prosecution, because the State must prove that you were a .08 BAC or above at the time you were driving, not at the time you submitted to the breath test.

◉ Was the Intoxilyzer properly calibrated and administered in accordance with FDLE Administrative Rules and Florida Statutes?

◉ Was the operator certified to use the equipment? We can obtain a detailed copy of the Intoxilyer's full maintenance records and discover any potential problems, malfunctions, or calibration issues associated with the machine. This could potentially prevent your breath test results from being lawfully introduced into court against you. The inadmissibility of breath test results can be very damaging to the prosecution and allow favorable negotiations directed toward the reduction of the charge or dismissal of your case.

# Seeking a Reduction Of Your DUI to Reckless Driving

**How the System Works – The Judge Can't Reduce Your DUI!**

In the United States, a criminal justice system is an "adversarial" system. This means that the results are driven by each party attempting to resolve the case in a manner that is consistent with his or her own best interest. In order to better understand how the process works, it is important to consider the roles of each party:

 It is the job of the police officer to establish "probable cause" and then make an arrest. It is not the job of the prosecutor to secure a conviction. More accurately, he/she is required to "seek justice." His/her obligation includes a thorough review of the police officer's investigation and a formal filing decision as to the most appropriate offense given the individual facts and circumstances of each case.

It is the job of the DUI defense lawyer to seek the best possible outcome for his client. This effort may include persuading the prosecutor to reduce the charge from DUI to Reckless Driving.

It is the job of the Judge to preside over the criminal court proceedings associated with the ultimate charge filed by the prosecutor. In that capacity, he/she is required to be equally fair to both the prosecution and the defense.

Thus, contrary to common misconceptions, it is not the Judge who has the authority or discretion to drop your DUI charge to Reckless Driving. Rather, only the prosecutor has the lawful ability to amend the charge. Therefore, it is critical to have an attorney who can effectively negotiate with the prosecutor when seeking a reduction of the DUI.

## How We May Seek a Reduction of Your DUI to Reckless Driving

*— Experience Matters —*

An experienced DUI defense attorney can thoroughly investigate the facts and circumstances of your DUI arrest to reveal every possible weakness in the prosecutor's case. Your attorney may be able to file motions with the court directed at suppressing admissible evidence. This can often have the effect of further weakening the State's case and provide you with an advantageous bargaining position to better secure a reduction of the charge.

*— A Team Approach to Pursuing a Reduction of Your DUI —*

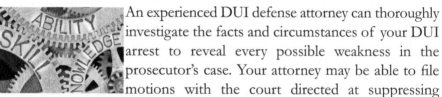

Attorneys Marc Pelletier and Tim Sullivan use a team approach when reviewing your video, police report, and all documentation associated with breath testing. This includes confirming the certification of the Intoxilyzer operator and reviewing the calibration of the breath testing device. As Former State Prosecutors, they personally reviewed hundreds of reduction requests. Both lawyers are certified Intoxilyzer operators. They have also received certification in proper field sobriety testing. Valuable experience in these two areas can be critical in effectively addressing any weaknesses in the State's evidence.

 If, after a thorough investigation, our office determines that your case is a suitable candidate for reduction, we will prepare detailed correspondence to the case assigned prosecutor in the Pinellas County State Attorney's Office.

It is important to outline all the deficiencies and weaknesses in the State's case:

◉ The facts associated with your driving and appearance on video are critical factors to address;

◉ Any applicable case law, legal arguments, procedural problems, and suppression issues affecting the admissibility of the evidence in your case must be leveraged;

◉ A complete analysis of the breath test machine, including the maintenance and calibration may strengthen our negotiating position;

◉ A review of the investigating law enforcement officer's background, integrity, and past performance via a public records request can shake the prosecutor's confidence in his/her own witness' testimony;

◉ Providing sworn affidavits by your passenger or other witnesses attesting to your sobriety and ability to safely operate the motor vehicle; and

◉ Highlighting any personal background information that could help show that the prosecutor's decision to amend your charge to Reckless Driving would be fair and equitable.

In the event a prosecutor's supervisor should later scrutinize the file, our reduction letter also serves as a permanent record that supports the decision of the case assigned prosecutor to reduce the charge.

As Former State Prosecutors, we are well aware that a detail oriented written argument for reduction can be a highly effective tool for achieving the best possible outcome.

## Why Would the Prosecutor Reduce Your DUI Charge to Reckless Driving?

 DUI charges that are amended to Reckless Driving very often carry DUI type sanctions. In other words, you may still have to attend DUI School, pay a fine, undergo an alcohol evaluation, and perform community service hours.

However, in return, you would not suffer a formal DUI conviction. The prosecutor benefits because he/she avoids the possibility of an acquittal had the demonstrably weak DUI case proceeded on to trial.

This plea bargain (i.e., a reduction of the charge but coupled with DUI type sanctions) is often viewed as an equitable "middle ground." In other words, if reduced, you do not suffer the stigma associated with a DUI conviction. But, at the same time, the prosecutor is assured that you get a valuable education on the perils of drinking and driving. He/she would likewise have confirmation that you do not suffer from addiction issues that could later subject you to another DUI arrest.

## Could My Case be a Good Candidate for a Reduction to Reckless Driving?

Every DUI case is different. At our free consultation, we can examine the following important aspects of your case:

- The lawfulness of the traffic stop;
- Whether the stop of your vehicle was based on driving that was indicative of impairment;
- Whether an accident or injury is involved;
- Whether any alcoholic beverage containers were discovered in your vehicle;
- Your performance on field sobriety testing;
- The legality of law enforcement's request for a breath, blood, or urine test;
- Whether you refused the breath, blood, or urine test;
- The test results, if you took a breath, urine, or blood test;

◉ The amount of time that elapsed from the time of driving to the time of testing; and

◉ Whether you behaved in a polite, cooperative, and respectful manner with law enforcement.

 When you meet with us, we will outline a plan of action that is designed to thoroughly investigate your case and uncover evidence that may be helpful to your defense.

## The Benefits of Getting a DUI Reduced to a Reckless Driving

*— Why a Reckless Driving Charge is Better than a DUI —*

◉ A DUI conviction, by law, will remain on your Florida DHSMV driving record for 75 years;

◉ A Reckless Driving conviction does not carry the same stigma associated with a DUI conviction;

◉ Your insurance company is likely to treat a Reckless Driving conviction in a far less critical manner than they would upon seeing your conviction for DUI. This could translate into saving thousands of dollars in increased insurance premiums. It might also prevent your insurance policy from being cancelled, or in the alternative, prevent you from being designated a high-risk driver;

◉ Getting your DUI reduced to Reckless Driving normally results in a lower fine than the minimum mandatory fine imposed for a DUI conviction;

◉ If your occupation entails driving in the course of your employment, a DUI conviction might result in your termination. On the other hand, your employer may be far more sympathetic and take a more favorable view of your case if the DUI charge was reduced to Reckless Driving;

◉ A DUI conviction on your driving record could jeopardize future applications for employment. Although your DUI conviction may not represent a felony, nor a crime involving untruthfulness or dishonesty, you could still be viewed by the potential employer as a liability risk; and

◉ If your current DUI case were to be reduced to Reckless Driving and you were later re-arrested for another DUI offense, you would still be considered a first time DUI offender. (Assuming you had no other DUI convictions.)

# Accidents

## Can I Be Arrested for DUI
## if the Other Motorist Caused the Accident?

Under Florida Law, it is not necessary that the prosecutor present any evidence of bad driving in order to seek a conviction for DUI. The State Attorney's Office need only show under Florida Statute Section 316.193 that you operated a vehicle (or were in actual physical control of a motor vehicle) while under the influence of an alcoholic beverage, a chemical substance listed in Florida Statute Section 877.111 or any substance controlled under Chapter 893. Further, that the alcoholic beverage, chemical or controlled substance affected you to the extent that your normal faculties were impaired.

## Being in the Wrong Place at the Wrong Time

Someone who has consumed alcohol could be exercising extreme caution in his/her efforts to safely drive home. Without committing any traffic infractions, he/she normally could not be lawfully stopped by a police officer for suspicion of DUI. However, his/her vehicle could be struck by an impaired driver and he/she is suddenly also subject an arrest for DUI. In other words, he/she was simply in the wrong place, at the wrong time. It can get much worse if someone dies as a result of the accident. In that situation, one or both drivers are likely to find themselves charged with the serious offense of DUI Manslaughter. That is because in Florida, it is not necessary to show that you "caused" the accident that led to the fatality. Only that in some way you "contributed" to the accident.

## What If I Am the At-Fault Driver?

 In cases where you are the at-fault driver, the State will seek to use the fact that an accident occurred as additional evidence that your normal faculties were impaired. In other words, the State will argue that the crash itself demonstrates that your ability to drive, judge distances, and react to road conditions was impaired by alcohol. Under these circumstances, it may be necessary to argue that the accident was unavoidable or caused by circumstances outside your control. For example, heavy fog, rain, or the actions of other drivers may have all played a role in causing the accident, rather than your consumption of alcohol.

Florida law has special provisions for DUI cases where a second vehicle was involved, but the car accident did not result in serious injury or death. These cases can be charged as "DUI with property damage" or "DUI with injury." A DUI involving property damage or non-serious injury is treated as a misdemeanor offense and the maximum penalty is up to one year in the county jail. Many Pinellas Judges require the completion of a "Victim Impact Panel" in addition to the other mandatory DUI penalties required by state law.

If your case involves an accident, you need the advice of an experienced DUI defense attorney. It is important for your attorney to examine the cause of the accident, the conditions on the roadway at the time, the potential witnesses to the collision, and the possibility that mechanical issues with your vehicle played a role. Investigating these issues may be helpful in building an argument that the accident was just that -- an accident -- and rebut the State's claim that your consumption of alcohol was to blame.

Beyond the facts and circumstances of the accident, additional procedural considerations may come into play. In many accident cases, Field Sobriety Tests are not conducted because the driver was transported from the scene to the hospital. A blood draw may have been secured because the taking of a breath test was "impossible or impractical." Therefore, the State's evidence may be limited to the test results rather than consist of video recorded Field Sobriety Tests or first-hand police observations of traffic infractions or unusual driving. Given this, the close scrutiny of the blood test results and the admissibility of this evidence is an effective strategy for defending your DUI case.

# Multiple Offenders

### What if This is Not My First DUI?

One of the first questions that our office asks when a new client comes to our firm for a consultation is whether they have ever previously been arrested for a DUI in Florida or any other state. Often times, we find clients initially answer no, despite the fact that they had previously been convicted for a DUI. When this conflict is discovered, clients often have similar explanations for the inconsistency:

◉ Well, that was 20 years ago, I didn't think it mattered;

◉ The officer did not document my prior conviction on the criminal arrest affidavit and instead wrote "No Priors";

◉ That was in Ohio, I thought you were only asking about Florida; or

◉ The name of the offense was not DUI, it was something else. (Other states refer to impaired driving offenses as DWI, DWAI, DUBAL, OVI, OWI, or OWAI.)

If you have ever previously been arrested for an offense involving the use of alcohol, controlled substances or chemical substances while operating a vehicle, your attorney needs to know. This information will have a tremendous impact on the strategy involved in your case. You should know that the State Attorney's Office will run an NCIC "Rap Sheet" on you during the discovery process. The purpose of an NCIC Rap Sheet is to ascertain an individual's *nationwide* record of arrests. Thus, if you have a prior DUI arrest, it is likely that the prosecutor will discover this while the case is pending.

### A Prior Offense and the DHSMV Administrative Process

In order to provide you with accurate advice as to the best method of navigating the DHSMV Administrative Suspension, it is important that your attorney know whether you have previously been charged with a DUI offense. As discussed previously, the "Waiver Process" is only available to the true first time offender. If you attempt to obtain a hardship license through the "Waiver Process" and have a previous DUI arrest, the DHSMV employee will first ask you if you have ever been arrested for a DUI in this or any other state. If you truthfully tell the employee of your prior DUI arrest, you will not be permitted to complete the "Waiver Process" as you are not considered a true first-time offender. On the other hand, if you fail to disclose your prior arrest to the DHSMV, you may have committed the felony offense of supplying false information in an effort to secure a driver's license.

If you have a prior DUI arrest, you will need to have your DUI defense team file a request for a Formal Administrative Review Hearing with the DHSMV Bureau of Administrative Reviews within 10 calendar days from your arrest. Therefore, it is of the utmost importance that you schedule an appointment with an experienced DUI defense lawyer right away.

# A Prior Offense and the Criminal Court Case

Under Florida Law, a prior conviction for DUI or a "similar offense" from another state serves as an aggravator to a new DUI charge. This can have significant repercussions on the penalties that might later be imposed if you are later convicted of the new DUI arrest.

Consider the following:

- If you were recently arrested for DUI, and were convicted of a DUI or similar offense within five years of the date of the new arrest, you will be facing enhanced penalties that include a five-year driver's license revocation and a minimum mandatory 10-day jail sentence;

- If you were recently arrested for a DUI, and have two prior convictions, one of which occurred within 10 years of the date of your new arrest, you will be facing enhanced penalties that include a ten-year driver's license revocation, and a minimum mandatory thirty-day jail sentence. In addition, the State may be able to file this new offense as a third-degree felony, rather than a misdemeanor.

- If this DUI constitutes your fourth or subsequent DUI offense, you are facing enhanced penalties that include a *lifetime* driver's license revocation. Moreover, if you were recently charged with a DUI and have three prior convictions for DUI or similar offenses, the State Attorney's Office may be able to file this new offense as a third-degree felony, regardless of how old your prior convictions are.

| Dept. of Highway Safety & Motor Vehicles, Div. of Driver's Licenses | | Criminal Court |
|---|---|---|
| | | **Minimum Mandatory Penalties Include:** |
| *Decision: 10 calendar days* | | DUI School, Alcohol Evaluation, Impoundment, Fines, Costs & Driver's License Suspensions: |
| **.08 and up** | **Refusal** | |
| • 1 X = 6 month admin. susp. | 1 X = 12 month admin. susp. | 1st DUI = 180 days - 1 year |
| • 2 X = 12 month admin. susp. | 2 X = 18 month admin. susp. | 2nd DUI w/in 5yrs = 5 years |
| *plus:* | | 2nd DUI not w/in 5yrs = 180 - 1 year |
| • 10 day driving ticket | *plus:* | 3rd DUI w/in 10yrs of 1st = 10 years |
| • 30 days "hard suspension" | 10 day driving ticket | 3rd DUI not w/in 10yrs of 1st and not w/in 5 years of 2nd = 180 days - 1 year |
| | 90 days "hard suspension" | 4th DUI = LIFE |
| 1st time offender: Eligible for Hardship D/L on Day 41 | 1st time offender: Eligible for Hardship D/L on Day 101 | Regardless of what happens at the DMV formal review hearing, it has **NO** effect on the outcome of your criminal court case. |

## How an Experienced DUI Defense Team May Be Able to Help

Certainly, the fact that you have a prior or multiple prior DUI arrests will make defending your case more difficult, in the sense that the State Attorney's Office is often less agreeable to reducing a charge where a defendant has one or more prior convictions for DUI. Nevertheless, it is imperative to immediately hire an experienced DUI defense team to begin working on your defense. Among the other issues addressed in earlier chapters, your attorney will need to investigate:

◉ Was the prior offense truly a "similar offense?" For example, if you were convicted for Driving With Alcohol in Your System, but not Driving While Impaired, it is likely that such a conviction could not be used to enhance your new DUI arrest;

◉ Can the State prove the existence of your prior DUI conviction? In general, in order to prove that a prior DUI conviction occurred, the State must obtain a certified copy of the "Judgment and Sentence" with fingerprints to establish that a conviction occurred and you were the person that was convicted. In some cases, those records are no longer available due to the age of the case or due to the record keeping policies for the jurisdiction where the offense occurred.

◙ Were you uncounseled at the time of your prior plea? The Florida Supreme Court has found that an uncounseled plea, for which the Defendant was indigent at the time and did not waive his or her right to an attorney, <u>may not</u> be used to enhance a misdemeanor to a felony.

If you have been charged with a DUI and have a prior arrest in your background, it is imperative that you inform your attorney of same. You want your attorney to be fully informed of the facts and circumstances of your case, and your background.

## Penalties – Am I Going to Jail?

The Florida Legislature has passed "mandatory minimum penalties" in DUI cases. This means that there are certain mandatory penalties that a Judge *must* impose upon conviction. The Judge has the power to impose sanctions that are more severe than just the minimums. However, the Judge may not impose sanctions that are less severe than those required, at a minimum, by the Florida Legislature.

Despite the existence of these mandatory minimums, there are still a number of methods for lessening the impact on your driver's license and your freedom. In some cases, we encourage our clients to complete the DUI school, alcohol evaluation, counseling and community service. This may result in reducing the time a person spends on probation (down to as little as one day). In other cases, we may have our client enter into a residential treatment program, which may be used as a substitute for any mandatory jail time pursuant to Florida Statute Section 316.193 (6)(m). Often, the Court may be persuaded to allow a "buy out" of the community service hours, rather than requiring an individual to complete the work.

Most first time DUI clients are eligible for a hardship license on the same day that they resolve their case in court, if they have completed DUI school in advance. The vehicle impound may be waived if an attorney demonstrates to the Judge that the impoundment would cause a hardship upon a third party.

As you can see, there are a number of "flexibilities" that are available despite the Florida Legislature's attempt to fashion standardized penalties in DUI cases. For this reason, it is imperative to obtain the services of an experienced DUI attorney who understands how the system works. Of course, obtaining a reduction of the DUI charge to Reckless Driving allows a person to avoid many of the mandatory sanctions that would otherwise be imposed.

### The Chart is a Start...But No Substitute for an Experienced Lawyer's Advice

We have outlined the mandatory penalties set forth by the Florida Legislature for your review. Given frequent changes to this area of the law by the Florida Legislature and the fact that every Pinellas County DUI case is different, readers are urged not to rely solely on graphs or charts. Our office can discuss with you whether your case may be a good candidate for a reduction to a lesser offense. Such an outcome could have the effect of side-stepping Florida's mandatory minimum DUI consequences and punishments under Florida Statute Sections 316.193(2), 316.193(3), and 316.193(4). For those clients with possible prior DUI convictions, we can counsel you on whether the prosecutor will discover your prior DUI conviction(s) and what impact it could have on your pending charge.

## PINELLAS COUNTY MANDATORY MINIMUM FLORIDA DUI PENALTIES

*(not including manslaughter or serious bodily injury)*

| TYPE OF DUI CHARGE | TOTAL AMOUNT OF FINES & COSTS | PROBATION PERIOD | DRIVER'S LICENSE REVOCATION PERIOD | JAIL TIME | VEHICLE IMPOUND | OTHER MANDATORY PENALTIES |
|---|---|---|---|---|---|---|
| 1st DUI BAC below .15 | $983.00 §316.193(2)(a) | 12 months §316.193(6)(a) | 6 months to 1 yr §322.28(2)(a)1 | Up to 6 months §316.193(2)(a)2.a | 10 days §316.193(6) (a-c) | DUI School Alcohol Evaluation & Treatment 50 hrs Community Service |
| 1st DUI BAC .15 or higher *or* person less than 18 yoa in car | $1,518.00 §316.193(4)(a) | 12 months §316.193(6)(a) | 6 months to 1 yr §322.28(2)(a)1 | Up to 9 months §316.193(4)(b)1 | 10 days §316.193(6) (a-c) | DUI School Alcohol Evaluation & Treatment 50 hrs Community Service 6 months ignition Interlock |
| 2nd DUI w/in 5 yrs. BAC below .15 | $1,518.00 §316.193(2)(a) | 12 months §316.193(6)(a | Mandatory 5 yrs §322.28(2)(a)2 | Mandatory 10 days §316.193(6)(b) Up to 9 months §316.193(2)(a)2.b | 30 days §316.193(6) (b) | Multiple Offender DUI School Alcohol Evaluation & Treatment 1 yr Ignition Interlock |
| 2nd DUI w/in 5 yrs. BAC .15 or higher *or* person less than 18 yoa in car | $2,558.00 §316.193(4)(a | 12 months §316.193(6)(a | Mandatory 5 yrs §322.28(2)(a)2 | Mandatory 10 days §316.193(6)(b) Up to 12 months §316.193(4)(b)2 | 30 days §316.193(6) (b) | Multiple Offender DUI School Alcohol Evaluation & Treatment 2 yrs ignition Interlock |
| 2nd DUI outside 5 yrs. BAC below .15 | $1,518.00 §316.193(2)(a) | 12 months §316.193(6)(a) | 6 months to 1 yr §322.28(1) | Up to 9 months §316.193(2)(a)2.b | 10 days §316.193(6) (a-c) | Multiple Offender DUI School Alcohol Evaluation & Treatment 1 yr Ignition Interlock |
| 2nd DUI outside 5 yrs. BAC .15 or higher *or* person less than 18 yoa in car | $2,558.00 §316.193(4)(a) | 12 months §316.193(6)(a) | 6 months to 1 yr §322.28(1) | Up to 12 months §316.193(4)(b)2 | 10 days §316.193(6) (a-c) | Multiple Offender DUI School Alcohol Evaluation & Treatment 2 yrs ignition Interlock |
| 3rd DUI w/in 10 yrs. BAC below .15 FELONY | $2,558.00 §316.193(4)(a) | Up to 60 months §775.082 | Mandatory 10 yrs §322.28(2)(a)3 | PCJ §316.193(6)(c) Up to 5 yrs State Prison §316.193(2)(b) §775.082(3)(d) | 90 days §316.193(6) (c) | Multiple Offender DUI School Alcohol Evaluation & Treatment 2 yrs ignition Interlock |
| 3rd DUI w/in 10 yrs. w/ BAC .15 or higher *or* person 18 yoa or less in car FELONY | $4,558.00 §316.193(4)(a) | Up to 60 months §775.082 | Mandatory 10 yrs §322.28(2)(a)3 | Mandatory 30days in PCJ §316.193(6)(c) Up to 5 yrs State Prison §316.193(2)(b) §775.082(3)(d) | 90 days §316.193(6) (c) | Multiple Offender DUI School Alcohol Evaluation & Treatment 2 yrs ignition Interlock |

| Offense | Fine | | License | Jail | Days | Requirements |
|---|---|---|---|---|---|---|
| 3rd DUI outside 10 yrs, BAC below .15 | $2,558.00 §316.193(2)(a) | 12 months §316.193(6)(a) | 6 months to 1 yr §322.28(1) | Up to 12 months §316.193(2)(b)2 | 10 days §316.193(6) (a-c) | Multiple Offender DUI School Alcohol Evaluation & Treatment 2 yrs Ignition Interlock |
| 3rd DUI outside 10 yrs w/BAC .15 or higher or person 18 yoa or less in car | $4,558.00 §316.193(4)(a) | 12 months §316.193(6)(a) | 6 months to 1 yr §322.28(1) | Up to 12 months §316.193(2)(b)2 | 10 days §316.193(6) (a-c) | Multiple Offender DUI School Alcohol Evaluation & Treatment 2 yrs Ignition Interlock |
| 4th DUI w/in lifetime FELONY | $3,015.00 (BAC >.15) or $4,558.00 (BAC .15+) §316.193(2)(b) | Up to 60 months §316.193(6)(a) §775.082 | Permanent §322.28(2)(e) | Zero or mandatory 10 or 30 days, or up to 5 yrs State Prison depending on age of prior DUI convictions §316.193(3) §775.082(3)(d) | 10, 30, or 90 days depending on age of prior DUI convictions §316.193(6) (a-c) | Multiple Offender DUI School Alcohol Evaluation & Treatment 2 yrs Ignition Interlock |

# What to Expect at Your Free Consultation

Initial consultations at our office are rather comprehensive. We recognize the complexity that this subject matter may present to a non-lawyer. For that reason, every effort has been made to deliver important information to our clients in an easy to understand manner. In that regard, when you visit our office you will begin your consultation by watching a short proprietary video from our "DUI Insider" series. This video was created by our DUI Defense Team to educate you on the crucial steps that need to be taken to protect your interest with both the DHSMV and the Pinellas County Criminal Court System. After you finish the video, you will have a face-to-face consultation with either Marc Pelletier or Tim Sullivan in our conference room. Both are highly experienced DUI defense attorneys. During this meeting, the attorney will encourage you to discuss your side of the story and the facts and circumstances that led to your arrest. This in-depth conversation will serve as the foundation for developing a strategy to best defend your case. While every case is different, you should expect that your attorney will make an inquiry into the following areas:

- Did the police have the lawful right to stop your vehicle?

- Are there any witnesses that might be beneficial to your defense?

- Did the officer properly administer field sobriety tests?

- Were the field sobriety tests conducted in a dry, level, and well-lit area?

- Did footwear such as high-heels, sandals, or flip flops negatively impact your performance of the testing?

- Were you at any time read your Miranda warnings?

- Do you suffer from any medical or physical issues that would inhibit your ability to perform sobriety exercises?

- Did you make any admissions to consuming alcohol?

- Did you have any alcohol beverage containers inside your vehicle?

- Did you make any admissions to consuming drugs or prescription medications?

- Were any drugs or prescription medications located on your person or in your vehicle?

- Were you polite, cooperative, and respectful to law enforcement?

- Did the police follow proper protocol when offering or administering the breath test?

- Did the police request a urine or blood test?

- Is there an allegation that you refused to submit to a breath, urine, or blood test?

- Was a "Drug Recognition Evaluation" performed in your case?

- Did you make any admissions to feeling impaired or admit that you should not have been operating a motor vehicle?

- Who is your arresting officer and is he experienced in conducting DUI investigations?

# Why Choose Us?

## We Made it <u>OUR</u> Business to Know Law Enforcement's Business

### We are Former State Prosecutors

We learned Street-level DUI enforcement tactics from the inside. We have first-hand knowledge of the strategies often used by the prosecution. Our experience provides us with the ability to identify potential areas of weakness. We believe that by having learned many of our adversary's tactics, we can provide you with insight and practical advice.

### Certified in Proper Roadside Field Sobriety Testing

Marc Pelletier is certified in field sobriety testing. Our office can review the video recording of your field sobriety tests to see if they were properly administered and interpreted fairly. Flawed field sobriety tests could lead to a reduced charge of Reckless Driving.

### Advised Law Enforcement Personnel at DUI Checkpoints

As Former State Prosecutors, attorney Tim Sullivan and attorney Marc Pelletier acted as on-site advisors to law enforcement on legal and procedural issues at DUI checkpoints. If your case involves a DUI roadblock, any deviation from court-approved procedures could jeopardize the State's case.

### We are Trained & Certified Intoxilyzer Operators

The outcome of your case could be influenced by your Intoxilyzer results. We will closely audit the operator's permit, the calibration records, and the machine's service history. Non-compliance with administrative rules or unexplained malfunctions could prohibit the admissibility of your test results in court.

### Intoxilyzer Inspector

Attorney Tim Sullivan was certified by the FDLE in the inspection & maintenance of the Intoxilyzer. His hands-on experience enables him to carefully review the alcohol wet bath solution protocol of this breath testing device. He can ascertain whether the police properly complied with Florida Law governing the calibration of the Intoxilyzer machine used in your case.

### We Own the Same Breath Testing Devices
### Used by Law Enforcement

Russo, Pelletier & Sullivan maintain the largest known, in-office, private collection of vintage and contemporary breath testing machines in the state of Florida. Clients learn that all breath testing machines have limitations and vulnerabilities.

### Completed "Masters of DUI" Program

Tim Sullivan and Marc Pelletier have both successfully fulfilled the requirements of the 2011 Masters of DUI Program offered through the Florida Bar's Continuing Education Program.

### Graduates of the National College for DUI Defense
### at Harvard Law School

Tim Sullivan and Marc Pelletier are graduates of the National College of DUI Defense at Harvard Law School. This course of instruction is generally regarded as providing the best advanced-level training in the art of DUI defense advocacy.

### NHTSA DUI Gold Standards Committee Member

Tim Sullivan and Marc Pelletier are honored to be two of only four private Pinellas County criminal defense lawyers selected to serve on the National Highway Traffic Safety Administration's "Pinellas County DUI Gold Standards Committee."

## Member of the DUI Defense Lawyers Association
Tim Sullivan is a member of the DUI Defense Lawyers Association. Of the thousands of lawyers who handle DUI cases in the State of Florida, only forty are members of this organization.

## Served as Adjunct Professor – DUI Program
In 2010, Timothy Sullivan served as an Adjunct Professor for the Florida Public Safety Institute's DUI Program at Tallahassee Community College.

## Completed DUI Drug Recognition Expert Course
Timothy Sullivan completed the same level of instruction as law enforcement in the proper detection of drug impaired drivers. He also lectured on this topic at a Florida Department of Transportation sponsored seminar.

## Instructor to Law Enforcement
## on DUI Detection and Enforcement
While serving as prosecutors, Tim Sullivan and Marc Pelletier lectured to law enforcement personnel on the proper methods associated with the detection and apprehension of impaired drivers.

## State Attorney's Agency Service Award
In 2003, Marc Pelletier was recognized for "Outstanding Performance and Service to the State Attorney's Office and the Citizens of Southwest Florida," 20th Judicial Circuit.

## Graduate of the Advanced DUI Seminar
Timothy Sullivan and Marc Pelletier are graduates of the Florida Prosecuting Attorney's Association continuing education program on advanced DUI litigation techniques. (Mr. Sullivan is a 2008 graduate, Mr. Pelletier is a 2004 graduate.)

# About Us

**Attorney Tim Sullivan**

Attorney Tim Sullivan has a wide-range of practical experience in the prosecution and defense of impaired drivers. His background includes a focus on the specialized and unique training the police rely upon in making a DUI arrest.

After graduating from college with honors, Tim went on to attend Stetson University College of Law. In addition to being recognized on the "Dean's List," Tim was also honored for his astute trial and evidence skills in Trial Advocacy Competitions.

As a law student, Tim gained valuable experience serving as a law clerk for a United States Federal Judge in Tampa. He also completed a clinical internship at our local State Attorney's Office in Pinellas County.

After graduating from law school, Tim was sworn in as a Pinellas County Assistant State Attorney. As a State prosecutor, Tim learned street-level DUI enforcement tactics from the inside. He quickly rose through the ranks in the State Attorney's Office and was selected to run the North County Criminal Traffic court division. Tim was promoted to "Lead Trial Assistant" and supervised other Assistant State Attorneys in the prosecution of countless DUI cases.

Tim has insight into the strategies often employed by both law enforcement and state prosecutors. He completed the same specialized DUI education and training undertaken by police officers assigned to the DUI squad. Tim is qualified to operate the Intoxilyzer 8000. However, his training did not end there. He went on to obtain "agency inspector" accreditation that enables him to conduct a thorough and in-depth review of the maintenance and calibration of the particular breath test machine used in your case.

Tim received a scholarship from the University of North Florida to attend the "DUI Drug Recognition Expert Program." There, he studied alongside DUI Squad Officers in the complex area of Drug-Impaired Driver detection.

Tim began training prosecutors at the Pinellas County Criminal Justice Center. Later, Tim was called upon to serve as an Adjunct Professor at Tallahassee Community College. In that capacity, he educated prosecutors from across the State about the potential vulnerabilities that can arise when prosecuting a DUI case.

In 2017, Tim was selected to the Florida Super Lawyers Magazine "Rising Star" list. This designation was bestowed upon Tim based upon peer recognition and professional achievement. Less than 2.5% of all Florida lawyers achieve the Super Lawyer, Rising Star distinction.

Tim has spent countless hours scrutinizing the maintenance and performance history of the Intoxilyzer machines used by all our local law enforcement agencies. He continually maintains and updates extensive files on each and every one of Pinellas County's Intoxilyzers. This dedicated effort can, at times, reveal critical problems with the calibration and reliability of the breath test machine used in your case.

Tim Sullivan's practical knowledge of his adversary's strategies and tactics, along with his command of the Intoxilyzer can translate into valuable insight used for the benefit of his clients in court.

Each year, Tim attends multiple seminars across the country to further his education in the area of DUI defense.

## Attorney Marc Pelletier

Attorney Marc Pelletier has considerable skill and in-depth knowledge of the criminal justice system. Marc graduated with honors from both Virginia Commonwealth University and Stetson College of Law. While at Stetson, he was recognized for his superior academic achievement in the areas of Criminal Sentencing Issues, Advanced Criminal Trial Advocacy and Appellate Practice.

He has worked for one of the largest law firms in the Southeast and clerked at the Virginia State Supreme Court. Marc was also employed by a criminal defense firm in Richmond, Virginia.

After being admitted to the Florida Bar, Marc served as a Assistant State Attorney. In addition to prosecuting violations of the law, Marc was responsible for lecturing police officers on DUI law. He was also an onsite advisor to law enforcement agencies concerning the complex legal issues that sometimes arose at DUI checkpoints. As a result of his commitment to the fair administration of justice, he later went on to receive the "Agency Service Award for Outstanding Performance and Service" in the execution of his duties while at the State Attorney's Office.

Marc's specialized credentials include certification as a breath test operator from the Florida Department of Law Enforcement and certification in the proper administration of field sobriety testing from the National Highway Traffic and Safety Administration. He has also completed Advanced

Continuing Legal Education Training in the areas of both DUI and criminal defense. Marc also received intensive continuing legal education at Harvard Law School's National College for DUI Defense.

The local criminal defense bar recognized Marc's experience and knowledge in the law by electing him to serve as the President of the Pinellas Association of Criminal Defense Lawyers for 2010-2011.

In 2016, the consumer lawyer rating organization www.AVVO.com honored Marc with its highest designation of "Superb." The rating organization found that "Marc Pelletier has been widely recognized by the legal community for superb professional conduct and experience."

As a member of the legal team at Russo, Pelletier & Sullivan, Marc's commitment to excellence and quality legal advocacy are an invaluable asset to the law firm. The law office of Russo, Pelletier & Sullivan is "AV" rated by Martindale-Hubbell. This 140-year-old company solicits attorney reviews from local lawyers and judges. An "AV" distinction is awarded only to law firms that display the highest level of skill, integrity, and ethical standards.

Made in the USA
Middletown, DE
26 March 2022

63166250R00046